Featured Recipes

Elegant Vanilla Yogurt with Fruit

4 cups whole milk
6 ounces plain whole milk yogurt
without added gelatin 3/4 c
1 tablespoon vanilla bean paste or
vanilla extract
Fresh fruit
Fresh herb garnish

Tip from Rhonda

Use fruit and garnish
of your choice.

Strawberries,
and blueberries
garnished with a sprig
of rosemary featured
here.

In a large sauce pan, with a thermometer attached, heat milk to 180°F. Maintain the 180°F temperature for at least 10 minutes. Remove the saucepan from heat and cool milk to 110°F. (This will take about 45 minutes.) Stir yogurt and vanilla bean paste into milk. Transfer milk mixture to a yogurt maker. Set fermentation time to 8 hours. Serve immediately or cover and store in the refrigerator for 3 to 5 days.

Canape of Lox

·Smoked salmon ·
Sliced pumpernickel bread
Organic cucumber
Fried or scrambled egg
Red or white onion
Tomato
Capers
Hot mustard
Lemon
Tarragon

Tip from Rhonda

Use a mandolin to slice
ingredients. Makes for a
beautiful presentation.

Note: Quantity of ingredients depends
on the number of guests being served.

Thinly slice cucumber, onion, tomato
and lemon. Cook egg any way you
prefer (scrambled here). Simply
assemble sandwich and garnish with
lemon and fresh herb of choice.

Spicy Guacamole

2 ripe ovocados
1 tomato
1/2 small red onion
fresh cilantro
1 lime
finishing or sea salt
japalena peppers to taste

Cut both avocados in half and scoop contents into a bowl. Finely chop onion, tomato and avocado, add to bowl. squeeze in the juice of the entire lime, add salt to taste. Use two forks or a potato masher to combine the ingredients. For a spicy kick, finely chop jalapeno or pepper of your choice. Transfer to a serving bowl per Rhonda's tip.

Tip from Rhonda

Serve with tortilla chips or quesadilla , salsa and sour cream.

Beet Salad

Sliced pickled beets
Sliced english cucumber
Multi-color cherry tomatoes
Goat cheese
Fresh dill

Simply layer ingredients in a pretty bowl and serve.

Tip from Rhonda

Serve with a poached salmon for a light and healthy meal.

Lobster Ravioli With Garlic Cream Sauce

Ravioli pasta
2 small lobster tails
1 tablespoon vegetable oil
1 cup fresh spinach (chopped)
2 cloves garlic minced
1/4 cup vegetable broth
1 cup heavy cream
1/2 teaspoon Worcestershire sauce
1/4 cup parmesan cheese
Salt
Pepper

Tip from Rhonda

Any pasta will do for this recipe. Be creative with your seafood as well.

Cook ravioli according to package instructions. Set aside. In a large cooking pan, heat oil then add chopped spinach. Sauté until spinach is soft. Add minced garlic, salt and pepper to taste. Cook for about 2-3 minutes or until garlic is fragrant. Add broth, heavy cream, and Worcestershire sauce, stir well. Add lobster tails. Stir occasionally. Add ravioli, carefully stir in and cook until lobster tails are done, approximately 10 minutes. Stir in parmesan cheese and cook for another minute or so. Serve immediately.

Steamed Lobster and Mussel Pot

Lobster tail
Mussels
Butter
Chopped Garlic
Chopped Onion
Lemon
White wine
Sea salt
Pepper

In a steaming pot, heat wine and the juice of lemon. Cover until liquids come to a rolling boil. Add lobster, mussels, onion, garlic, sliced lemon, sea salt, pepper, and butter. Cover pot and let steam until lobster is red and mussel shells are open. Reduce wine mixture, toss seafood until coated. Serve immediately.

Tip from Rhonda

Very simple recipe that can be prepared for one or a group. Adjust quantity of seafood accordingly.

Big Mac Eggrolls

1 pound ground beef
2 cups cooking oil
1 pack egg roll wrappers
1/3 cup shredded lettuce
1/3 cup diced sour pickles
1/3 cup American cheese
1 medium coarsely
chopped white onion
1 garlic clove, chopped
1 tablespoons sesame seeds
2 tablespoons cooking oil
Seasonings to taste (salt,
pepper, garlic powder,
onion salt)
1 tablespoon mayonnaise
1 tablespoon ketchup
1 tablespoon sweet pickle
relish
1 tablespoon mustard

Tip from Rhonda

Make a big batch.
Can be frozen raw or
cooked.

In a cast iron skillet, brown ground beef in oil 1 tablespoon of cooking oil, adding onions, garlic and seasoning to taste. At the end of cooking, stir in pickles and cheese until melted. Allow mixture to cool before filling and wrapping liberal amounts into egg roll wrappers. Bring remainder of cooking oil to a rolling boil and fry rolls until golden brown Remove and let drain on paper towel. Sprinkle with sesame seeds while still hot Begin the special sauce by simply combining mayonnaise, ketchup sweet pickle relish and mustard into a bowl, adjusting ingredients to taste. Serve rolls over shredded lettuce.

Spicy Guacamole

2 ripe ovocados
1 tomato
1/2 small red onion
fresh cilantro
1 lime
finishing or sea salt
japalena peppers to taste

Cut both avocados in half and scoop contents into a bowl. Finely chop onion, tomato and avocado, add to bowl. squeeze in the juice of the entire lime, add salt to taste. Use two forks or a potato masher to combine the ingredients. For a spicy kick, finely chop jalapeno or pepper of your choice. Transfer to a serving bowl per Rhonda's tip.

Tip from Rhonda

Serve with tortilla chips or quesadilla , salsa and sour cream.

Cheesy Lasagna

2 pounds ground beef/chicken/pork/beyond beef
1 box lasagna noodles
2 large cans of Manwich sauce
2 cups of assorted cheeses
1 large onion 1 clove garlic
1 large green bell pepper
Fresh or dried basil
Fresh or dried oregano
1 tablespoon cooking oil
To taste salt, pepper, onion ,powder, nutmeg

In a sauce pan, heat cooking oil until moderately hot. Add protein, basil, oregano, chopped onion, garlic, and bell pepper. Season with salt, pepper, onion powder and nutmeg. Cook thoroughly adding Manwich sauce at the end. Stir to incorporate all ingredients, turn down heat to simmer. Meanwhile, boil the lasagna noodles until fork tender, drain and set aside to cool. Layer noodles, cheese and sauce in a shallow pan. Bake in a 350 degrees oven for 30 to 45 minutes.

Tip from Rhonda

Be creative with your ingredients. The sky in the limit with this recipe.

Salt and Pepper Fried Lobster Tail

Tip from Rhonda

Make this as mild or as spicy as you like. I like it hot!

2 pound spiney lobster tail
1/3 cup habanero peppers chopped
1/3 cups chili peppers chopped
1 egg whipped with 1 teaspoon water
1 cup cooking oil
2 tablespoons flour
Butter lettuce
Sliced lemons
Hot habanero honey
Seasonings to taste (course sea salt, course ground pepper, garlic salt, and onion powder)

Remove lobster meat from shell, devein, and rinse. Cut into fairly large chunks. Lightly season. He at oil to a medium boil Dip pieces of l obster into the egg and water mixture, lightly coat with flour and fry until lightly brown. Add peppers 30 second prior to removing the lob ster from the oil. Into a large metal bowl, add course sea salt and ground pepper.

Swirl around until lightly coated Remove from bowl and plate at op-butter lettuce.Drizzle with habanerohoneyandgarnishwith lemon slices.

Crispy Fried Lobster

2 pound spiney lobster tail
1 egg whipped with1 teaspoon water
1 cup cooking oil
2 tablespoons flour
butter lettuce
sliced lemons
Seasoning to taste (course sea salt,
course ground pepper, garlic salt,
onion powder)

Tip from Rhonda

Serve with sticky rice
and have fun with it,
use chop sticks.

Remove lobster meat from shell, devein, and rinse. Cut into fairly large chunks. Season. Heat oil to a medium boil. Dip pieces of lobster into the egg and water mixture. Lightly coat with flour and fry in the oil until lightly brown. Drain pieces of lobster on paper towel. Plate atop butter lettuce and garnish with lemon slices.

Sticky Pork Belly

½ pound pork belly
4 cups water 4 slices of fresh ginger 1
small diced onion
2 cloves of crushed garlic
2 tablespoons cooking oil
2 tablespoons brown sugar
3 tablespoons light soy sauce
3 tablespoons dark soy sauce
3 tablespoons rice wine
1/3 pound Bok choy cooked rice

Cut the pork belly into roughly 1inch cubes. Bring 1 liter of water to a boil in a sauce pan, add the pork, ginger, onion, and garlic, and cook for 3 to 4 minutes. Remove pork from the water using a slotted spoon and drain on a plate lined with a paper towel. Discard the remaining water and vegetables. Clean and dry the pot, return it to high heat and add the olive oil. Return the pork to the pan and cook until browned. The oil may pop and splatter, so be careful.

For the sticky sauce, incorporate brown sugar, water, light soy sauce, dark soy sauce, 2 minced garlic, 2 slices of ginger, ½ teaspoon of black pepper, and salt.
Stir everything together and let it cook for a minute or two. Add pork until well coated. Serve with rice and steamed bok choy.

Tip from Rhonda

This dish is a labor of love but well worth it.

Traditional Filipino Lumpia

1 tablespoon vegetable oil
1 pound ground pork
2 cloves garlic, crushed
½ cup chopped onion
½ cup minced carrots
½ cup chopped green onions
½ cup thinly sliced green cabbage
1 teaspoon ground black pepper
1 teaspoon salt
1 teaspoon garlic powder
1 teaspoon soy sauce
30 lumpia wrappers
2 cups vegetable oil for frying

Tip from Rhonda

Serve with dipping sauces such as duck sauce, hot mustard, sweet chili and soy.

Place a wok or large skillet over high heat, and pour in 1 tablespoon vegetable oil. Cook pork, stirring frequently, until no pink is showing. Remove pork from pan and set aside. Drain grease from pan, leaving a thin coating. Cook garlic and onion in the same pan for 2 minutes. Stir in the cooked pork, carrots, green onions, and cabbage. Season with pepper, salt, garlic powder, and soy sauce. Remove from heat, and set aside until cool enough to handle. Place three heaping tablespoons of the filling diagonally near one corner of each wrapper, leaving a 1 1/2 inch space at both ends. Fold the side along the length of the filling over the filling, tuck in both ends, and roll neatly. Keep the roll tight as you assemble. Moisten the other side of the wrapper with water to seal the edge. Cover the rolls with plastic wrap to retain moisture. Heat a heavy skillet over medium heat, add oil to 1/2 inch depth, and heat for 5 minutes. Slide 3 or 4 lumpia into the oil. Fry the rolls for 1 to 2 minutes, until all sides are golden brown. Drain on paper towels. Serve immediately.

Grilled Chicken Veggie Soup

4 pounds chicken
2 tablespoon cooking oil
2 cups vegetable broth
2 cups chicken stock
3 cups coarsely chopped onion
1 large garlic clove, chopped
10 ounces of kale
1/2 cup baby carrots
10 stalks asparagus
1/4 pound of petite red potatoes
2 cans small white beans
2 tablespoons flour
1 stick of butter
2 tablespoons olive oil
Seasonings to taste (sea salt,
pepper, garlic salt, and paprika

Tip from Rhonda

Delicious served with
honey butter corn bread.

Chop chicken into one inch cubes, season and sauté in cooking oil until brown, set aside. . In a large pot over medium high heat, melt butter. Whisk in flour and stir constantly until flour is completely incorporated. Add chicken and beef stock, continuing to whisk vigorously until well incorporated. Add seasonings to taste and set aside. Cut vegetables to desired size, season with salt and pepper, toss in olive oil. Spread veggies out on baking sheet, preferably grated cast iron for the best flavor. Place in a 400 degree oven, observing closely, turning as necessary. Heat soup, toss in chicken and roasted vegetable. Bring to a boil, remove the vegetable from oven and add directly to the pot. Add beans directly to the pot, no need to drain. Reduce heat and let soup simmer for at least 30 minutes.

Louisiana Style Gumbo

1 pound andouille sausage
1 pound shrimp, peeled and deveined
2 cups chicken stock
3 cups coarsely chopped onion
1 large garlic clove, chopped
1/2 cup baby carrots5 stalks m of celery
1/3 cup green onions
2 tablespoons flour
2 tablespoons cooking oil
Seasonings to taste (sea salt, pepper, garlic salt, cajun seasoning)

Tip from Rhonda

Be creative with ingredients. Try chicken or any other protein or vegetable.

In a large pot, combine flour and oil and cook, stirring constantly on medium low heat. It is important to stir constantly so that it doesn't burn it. But you do want a deep dark color. The darker the roux, the deeper the flavorAdd chicken broth to the roux and stir well. Season to taste and turn the heat down to medium lowChop onions, peppers, celery, carrots, and add to the pot and cook for one hourTransfer mixture to a crock pot, add shrimp and andouille sausage. Cook low and slow for two hoursServe with white rice and honey butter cornbread

Surf and Turf

1 steak of choice Seasonings to taste (salt, pepper, garlic salt, paprika, and nutmeg)
1/2 pound. Jumbo lump crab meat
1/4 cup chopped parsley
3/4 cup Ritz crackers, crushed
3/4 teaspoon Worcestershire sauce
3/4 teaspoon lemon juice
3/4 teaspoon Phillips Seafood Seasoning
3/4 teaspoon Dijon mustard
1/2 cup mayonnaise
1 large egg

For the crab cake, combine the egg, Worcestershire sauce, lemon juice, seafood seasoning, Dijon mustard and mayonnaise in a bowl. Place the crab meat, parsley and Ritz crackers into a separate bowl. Mix very lightly to combine. Add the wet ingredients to the crab mixture and combine lightly. Portion into 5-ounce cakes and pan fry or bake at 375°F for 12-15 minutes or until evenly browned on both sides and cakes reach an internal temperature of 165° F.

For the steak, season to taste. Heat a cast iron skillet with the teaspoon of olive and grill steak on each side to preferred temperature. (This will depend on the size and thickness of the steak). Serve with fries, aioli, tarter or creamy horseradish shown. Garnish with lemon wedge

Tip from Rhonda

Served here with fries and creamy horseradish for dipping.

BBQ Braised Oxtail Chili

6 pounds oxtails
1/2 cup flour for dredging the oxtail
6 tablespoons cooking oil
3 cups finely chopped onion
3 large garlic cloves, minced
1 tablespoon grated peeled fresh gingerroot
2/3 cup firmly packed light brown sugar
1 1/2 cups ketchup
3 tablespoons Dijon-style mustard
1 cup cider vinegar
1/4 cup Worcestershire sauce
1/4 cup lemon juice
Tabasco to taste cayenne to taste a 28-ounce can Italian tomatoes, drained, reserving the juice, and chopped
2 cans white small white beans
Seasonings to taste (salt, pepper, garlic salt, paprika, and nutmeg)

Tip from Rhonda

Make this for your next chili cook-off. I won first place.

Season oxtails liberally with salt, pepper, garlic salt, paprika and nutmeg, set aside. Add cooking oil cast iron skillet. Heat should be moderately high. Dredge oxtails in flour and add to the skillet and gook to golden brown, then transfer to plate. Add the remaining 2 tablespoon of oil into the skillet. In it cook the onion, the garlic, and the gingerroot over moderately low heat, stirring, until the onion is softened, and stir in the brown sugar, the ketchup, the mustard, the vinegar, the Worcestershire sauce, the lemon juice, the Tabasco, the cayenne, the tomatoes with the reserved juice, and salt and seasoning to taste. Transfer the mix to a crock pot and cook on low for 4 hours. Drain the beans well and stir them into the oxtail mixture. Cook on high for an additional hour.

Oxtail Stew

3 pounds Oxtails (cut into segments by a butcher) add Kosher Salt to taste Black Pepper (freshly ground) 3 tablespoons Light Brown Sugar 2 Spanish Onions (peeled and chopped) 4 cloves Garlic (peeled and minced) 3 tablespoons Fresh Ginger (peeled and chopped) 1 Scotch Bonnet Pepper (whole) 3 sprigs Fresh Thyme 12 Allspice Berries 1 bunch Scallions (trimmed and chopped) 2 tablespoons White Sugar 3 tablespoons Soy Sauce 1 tablespoon Worcestershire Sauce 3 tablespoons Flour 3 tablespoons Tomato Ketchup

Tip from Rhonda

A dollop of rice and that's all she wrote!

Season oxtails aggressively with salt and pepper. Heat a large Dutch oven or a heavy-bottomed pot over high heat. Add brown sugar to pot and melt, stirring with a wooden spoon, until it darkens and starts to smoke -- about six minutes. When sugar is nearly black, add 2 tablespoons boiling water. (It will splatter.) Stir to mix.Add the oxtails to the pot, working in batches, stirring each time to cover them with blackened sugar, then allowing them to cook, turning occasionally, until they are well browned. Remove oxtails to a bowl and keep warm.Add half of the onions, garlic and ginger to the pot, along with the pepper, the thyme, the allspice and a third of the scallions, and stir to combine. Allow to cook until softened, approximately 5 minutes.Return the oxtails to the pot along with any accumulated juices and put water into the pot so that the oxtails are almost submerged. Bring to a simmer and then cook, covered, approximately 1 hour, stirring occasionally.

Add remaining onions, garlic and ginger to the pot, along with another third of the scallions. Add sugar, soy sauce and Worcestershire sauce. Stir to combine and continue to cook until the meat is yielding and loose on the bone, approximately one hour longer. Remove approximately one cup of liquid from pot and place in a small bowl. Add flour to this liquid and stir to combine, working out any lumps with the back of a spoon. Add this slurry to the pot along with ketchup, then stir to combine and allow to cook a further 15 minutes or so. Remove Scotch bonnet pepper and thyme stems. Fold butter beans into the stew and allow these to heat through. Scatter remaining scallions over the top. Serve with white rice or rice and peas.

Pancake Batter Wings

10 chicken wings
1/2 cup pancake mix of choice
jalapino peppers
hot honey
flour
2 cups of cooking oil
salt
pepper
paprika
nutmeg

Tip from Rhonda

Wings were used here but thighs, legs breast meat and tenders may be used as well.

Wash fresh chicken wing and dry thoroughly with paper towel. Season liberally with spices. set aside and prepare pancake batter according to package instructions, adding more liquid to make a slightly thinner mix. Heat cooking oil in a skillet (preferably cast iron). Dip wing in batter and add to skillet. Oil should sizzle. Fry wings until golen brown. Remove from skillet and drain on paper towel. Transfer to a serving dish and drizzle with a hot or habanero honey.

Crab Bechamel Linguini

1 1/2 cup chicken broth
1 tablespoon grated onion
Dash of thyme and nutmeg
1/2 cup butter
1/2 cup flourl
2 cup milkl
2 cup cream
1 cup sliced mushrooms
2 egg yolks
2 cups crabmeat
Dash of cayenne pepper Salt
and pepper to taste

Tip from Rhonda

Any type of seafood or pasta can be substituted in this recipe. Let your imagination flow.

Make Mushroom Bechamel Sauce Combine chicken broth, 1 teaspoon grated onion, few grains of thyme, few grains of nutmeg. Bring to boil; reduce heat and simmer for 20 minutes. Strain and measure. Add water if necessary to make 1 cup. SautÃ mushrooms in 1/4 cup butter for 5 minutes. Add 1/4 cup four and stir until well blended. Remove from heat and cook, stirring constantly, until thick and smooth. Add cream, cayenne pepper, salt and pepper. Makes about 2 cups. Stir a little of the hot sauce into slightly beaten egg yolks. Stir in remaining sauce. Add 3 cups crabmeat. Stir over low heat until well heated. Serve in croustades, patty shells or timbale cases. Or, turn into greased scallop shells or individual ramekins; sprinkle with buttered crumbs and paprika and brown in a hot oven or under broiler. Makes about 6 servings.

Korean Braised Short Ribs

Merinade

soy sauce sugar (brown or white)
garlic rice vinegar green onions
sesame or vegetable oil

1 cup soy sauce
½ cup brown sugar
½ cup water
3-5 cloves garlic minced
2 tablespoons rice vinegar
3 green onions chopped
¼ cup sesame or vegetable oil
5 pounds Korean-style short ribs
cut across bones

Tip from Rhonda

The second most important trick to making amazing Grilled Korean Short Ribs is the marinade. It should be savory, with a slight tang and a full, rich flavor.

In a large zip lock bag, combine together the soy sauce, brown sugar, water, garlic, green onions and sesame oil to dissolve sugar. Add ribs, squeeze out all the air and refrigerate for 4 hours or overnight. Preheat outdoor grill for medium-high heat and lightly oil the grate. Remove the ribs and discard the marinade. Grill until meat is medium rare, about 3 minutes per side.

Crispy Air Fryer Wings

Fresh chicken wings
flour
light cooking oil
salt
pepper
garlic salt
nut meg
dry mustard

Wash an thoroughly with paper towel. Season liberally in a bowl with spices. Massage in a very light amount of oil into the wings. On the chicken setting or 350 degrees on your air fryer, cook for approximately 20 minutes. Remove when chicken is crispy and golden.

Tip from Rhonda

These wings can also be made naked, meaning without oil or flour.

Easy One Pot Steamed Seafood Feast

1/2 lb. each of:
Shrimp
Crawfish
mussels
1 whole clove of minced garlic
1/2 stick of butter
1 sliced lemon
1.2 small red onion
2 boiled eggs
2 small potatoes
peppers of choice (optional)
salt
pepper
Old Bay seasoning

Boil potatoes until soft, and eg until hard boiled (approx. 8 minutes). Thoroughly clean all seafood, ensuring mussels are closed and shrimp are deveined. Add water, stock, white wine, or beer to the bottom of the steam pot and cover until steam emits. add all ingredient to the steamer at once, and cover.

Tip from Rhonda

Old Bay hot sauce tastes amazing with this dish.

Fresh White Wine Butter Mussels

2 lbs. Mussels
Butter
Chopped Garlic
Chopped Onion
Lemon
White wine
Tomato
Sea salt
Pepper

In a steaming pot, heat wine and the juice of lemon. and cover until liquids come to a rolling boil. Add lobster, mussels, onion, garlic, sliced lemon, sea salt, pepper, and butter. Cover pot and let steam until mussel shells are open, add diced tomato. Reduce wine mixture and toss seafood until coated.

Tip from Rhonda

Serve with a crusty to mop up all if that flavorful butter, garlic, white wine sauce.

Yum Yum Shrimp

2 lbs. shrimp
2 tbspn flour
1 egg
salt
pepper
garlic salt
paprika
2 cups cooking oil
shredded lettuce

Peel and devein shrimp. thoroughly dry and lightly season with spices. Hear cooking oil in a skillet until moderately hot. Mix egg with one tablespoon of water. dip shrimp in mixture and then lightly coat with flour. Add shrimp to skillet one at a time to prevent them from sticking together. Fry to a light golden brown. Remove from skillet and dry on a rack or paper towel. Transfer to a bowl and coat with the yum yum sauce of your choice. Serve over shredded lettuce.

Tip from Rhonda

I serve Oriental style with chop sticks.

Simply Ribs

2 lbs. of ribs
2 tbsp. cooking oil
salt
pepper
paprika
onion powder
dried mustard
nutmeg

This recipe is more about the cooking technique and how to get moist, flavorful ribs while achieving a good char.

Wash dry and season ribs (any ribs) liberally with spices.

Rub with cooking oil and let sit for 30 minutes to marinate.

Use a heavy cast iron, grated skillet. Heat it in the oven on 400 degrees until very hot.

Add ribs and let grill until done, flipping ribs several times.

Using your favorite BBQ sauce, homemade or store bought, sauce the under side of the ribs and let bake for 10 to 15 minutes. Flip and sauce the main side (as pictured) and grill face down for another 10 to 15 minutes.

Best ribs you'll eat from an oven!

Tip from Rhonda

Oven temperature and cooking times will vary depending on the thickness of the meat and your oven.

Naked Salt and Pepper Wings

1 lb. Drummets
2 cups. cooking oil
1/2 small white onion
1/2 clove of garlic minced
assorted peppers of choice
salt
pepper
paprika
onion powder
dried mustard
nutmeg

Wash and thorougly dry chicken. Season with spices to taste. heat oil, preferably in a wok. Fry chicken until crispy and golden brown. Remove chicken and drain all but a tablespoon of oil. heat the oil on high heat and add peppers, onions, and garlic to flash fry. After about 30 seconds return the wings to the pan and toss to coat. Transfer to a serving dish without draining.

Tip from Rhonda

Have plenty of napkins handy. These wings are finger lickin' good!